A Noise
in the Woods

"God who guards you never sleeps"

Psalm 121:3

Karyn Henley

A Noise in the Woods

"Whoo-oo-oo is ready to go camping?" asked Owlfred.

"Me!" said Twigs. "I'm bringing my teddy bear."

"I'm ready too!" said Chester. "I'm bringing games to play!"

"I think I'm ready," said Mimi. "I've brought my palette and brushes."

"And I've packed lots of camping snacks," said Mrs H.

"I'm always ready," said Tennyson, dusting off his shell. "I carry my sleeping bag wherever I go!"

"Wonderful!" said Owlfred. "Everyone follow me. I know just the place to go!"

The Tails friends followed Owlfred past the pond.

They hiked through the woods until they came to a clearing.

"Here it is," said Owlfred. "How do you like it?"
"It's perfect," said Mrs H. She began to unpack the snacks.

Twigs helped Chester build a campfire, while Mimi drew a picture of wildflowers. Then Chester led everyone in a game of Follow the Leader and Hopscotch.

By that time, it was getting late.
Mrs H had steaming cups of
cocoa ready for everyone.

So they all sat around the campfire and sipped their cocoa and shared stories.

"I have a song for this occasion," said Tennyson.

"The silver moon climbs higher and higher,
and here we sit around the fire,
relaxing now as daytime ends,
here we are, the best of friends."

Everyone clapped. But Tennyson's eyes opened wide. "What was that sound?" he asked. Everyone listened.

Owlfred laughed. "Those are only night bugs," he said.

"Oh," said Tennyson. "Only night bugs."

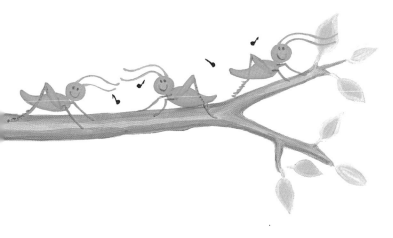

Tennyson led everyone in another song. Then he said, "Shh! What was that?" It was a scratchy, chirpy sound.

Owlfred laughed. "Those are only crickets, my friend," he said.

"Oh," said Tennyson. "Only crickets."

Chester stretched and yawned. "I'm sleepy," he said. "It must be bedtime."

One by one, the friends began to yawn. Everyone agreed that it was time to go to sleep. Everyone except Owlfred. "I sleep in the daytime," said Owlfred. "If I ever sleep at night, it's only a nap."

"Good!" said Tennyson. "Then you can stay awake and keep watch for us. All these night sounds make me quite nervous."

"I'll be happy to watch," said Owlfred.
He flew up into a nearby tree so he
could keep a good look out.

Everyone else settled down to sleep. But it wasn't long before Tennyson heard a rumbly tumbly sound. "Listen!" whispered Tennyson. Everyone was quiet. They all peered out into the darkness.

The low rumbly sound came again. This time there was a whistling sound with it. "What is it, Mum?" asked Twigs, squeezing a little closer to Mrs H.

"Don't worry," said Mrs H. "I'm sure Owlfred is watching, and he'll let us know if there is something to worry about."

The rumbly tumbly sound came again, even louder. Everyone dived into their sleeping bags.

In a minute, Chester peeked out and looked around. Then he whispered, "Look! Over there!" He pointed up into a tree.

Tennyson looked. "It's Owlfred!" he exclaimed. "Shhh!" said Mimi. "He's taking a little nap."

"If Owlfred's taking a nap, who will watch over us?" asked Twigs.

"God will watch over us," said Mrs H. "Remember: God who guards you never sleeps."

"That's right," said Chester. "Besides, with that snore, Owlfred will scare away anything that might try to bother us."

"You're right!" said Tennyson. He yawned and pulled himself into his shell. "Good night!" he called in his echoey voice.

"Good night!" everyone called back as they settled down and closed their eyes.

And all of them slept quite soundly all night long. Even Owlfred!

"God who guards you never sleeps"

Psalm 121:3